1-8
B
THE MA

Legacy Bible

Floor construction —

Key Cristopher —
Lindsey mass
3 children shirt
Marity Hickey

Audrey — 1-800-627-1995
1-800 Bible in my
plumbing

1 (917) 626 - 6035

Anne

Angus

II - Hebredes Island
Coast of Scat
Island of Lewis
Aunt Irene —

GEORGE LOW

THE MASTER OF PUTTING

with AL BARKOW

Middle East

Captagon —

Massive —

awake —

super

Terrorist

L&B

LYONS & BURFORD, PUBLISHERS

True View Foundation —

280 Vineyard Lane

Eutaw, Alabama

35462

Photographs in the chapter "The Styles of the Best" are used
with permission of UPI/Corbis-Bettmann (pages 74, 76, 78, 81, 82).
Photographs on page 84 and all photographs in the preceding
chapters are by Al Barkow.

Printed in the United States of America

10 9 8 7 6 5 4 3 2 1

Library of Congress Cataloging-in-Publication Data

Low, George, 1912–
    The master of putting / George Low with Al Barkow.
        p. cm.
            Originally published: New York: Atheneum, 1983.
            ISBN 1-55821-524-7
            1. Putting (Golf)   I. Barkow, Al.   II. Title.
        GVS79.P8L68   1997   96-39940
        796.352'35—dc21   CIP

CONTENTS

Shamanism

Buddhism

In George Low's view of the world, the measure of a successful man is whether or not he owns an overcoat. If he does, he isn't. In short, people who are "making it" take their winters in warm climes, just as George always does. This is remarkable if only because, as Low himself says, he hasn't worked for seventy years (his age at this writing). Not that Low is independently wealthy, understand. He must earn his daily steak and ale, and he always has. Indeed, there was a time, however brief, when he did so more or less "on the legit" as a club professional, sometimes tour player, owner of a small Florida fishing fleet. And, over the years, he has collected some royalties from the sale of George Low signature-model putters. None of these required the lifting of anything heavy, of course, and, therefore, cannot be classified as work.

In any case, Low's preferred way to live is from day to day, independent of anyone else's wishes, even if they happen to be picking up the check. In other words, George lives by his wits. It is the way of the master putter, if you please. Great ball strikers—big hitters off the tee, strong iron-players—tend to be indifferent putters, and also less interesting personalities. They seem to feel the world is a simply structured place where you gain dominance by force, power, sheer strength. They are the artillery men, who think wars are won merely by long-range destruction.

Good putters, on the other hand, are apt to be keener of mind, more attuned to the subtleties of life. In our military metaphor they are the ones who do the final, real work of war. After the artillery shelling has ceased, the putters move in to deal with the intricacies of the occupation. When the shelled come out from the rubble they are angry, resentful, and need to be coaxed into co-operation, which is the final, ultimate defeat.

In terms of George Low's life-style, we are talking about such things as figuring the speed of a race horse at a particular short interval of time—the shorter the better. Or, the athletic ability of other horses that do not necessarily eat grass, such as those who toss balls around or hit them with various kinds of sticks. In the latter instance, Low might have some direct influence, and indirect participation. If Low feels he has "done the guy some good," those who come to him for putting help may afterward become the object of their mentor's wagers. More often than not he has done them some good.

For example, a couple of winters ago one Joel Hirsch, an amateur golfer from Chicago, went to Florida for a standard three-day set of putting lessons from the master, for which he paid Low the usual fee. A few months later Hirsch rose out of virtual competitive obscurity (in national/international golf; he has long been a fine competitor in his hometown) to reach the finals of the British Amateur Championship (which he lost). Hirsch made no bones about Low's contribution to his success.

But let us take this back even further, and with considerably more celebrity. After Arnold Palmer won his second Masters title, in 1960, with crucial putts holed on the last two greens, he told the press, "The only thing I did on those two putts was keep thinking of what my friend, George Low, always says, 'Keep your head down, and don't move.' "

By all means, Low always puts his money on his own putting ability. It has been many years now since he quit that so-called hustle, but his success in this arena underlies much of his legend. It included putting, not only with the sort of stick everyone else uses, but with bottles or canes, kicking the ball, using whatever seemed an unlikely instrument for the business. Not that George couldn't play the rest of the game. When Byron Nelson's famous and fabulous streak of tournament victories was snapped at eleven straight, in the 1945 Memphis Open, the winner of the event was Freddie Haas, Jr., then an amateur golfer. The low professional was George Low, who at thirteen under par (275) was five behind Haas and one shot ahead of Nelson. Sam Snead, by the way, was at 280.

If Low could play so well, why didn't he pursue a tournament career? His most recent response to this is "I performed a minor miracle in Memphis, and got twenty-eight hundred. Does that tell you anything?"

Paul Grossinger, owner of a famous resort in the Catskill Mountains of New York, once dubbed Low "America's Guest." Which is to say, not all Low's living has come in the form of direct exchanges of money. There is a sort of barter system by which he also operates, and which he has always found more challenging. "There ain't no point in loafing with a broke," Low once told sportswriter Dan Jenkins, "because nothing falls off." Being a man of his word, Low has loafed with the best, from Eisenhower to Sinatra, and with a lot of very successful businessmen in between.

And what does George provide in return for rent-free lodging, the occasional meal on the house, tickets to sporting events, a ride from here to there?

Well, now . . .

Low's father, George, Sr., was one of the first Scots-born golf professionals to emigrate to the United States when the game was introduced here. Low, Sr., who reputedly coined the all-too-true phrase "Golf is a humblin' game," had a long and distinguished career in his adopted country. For over twenty-five years he was head professional at the prestigious Baltusrol Golf Club, in New Jersey. He taught two presidents about niblicking—Taft and Harding—and was a force in the formation and development of the Professional Golfers Association (PGA) of America. Low, Sr., was also a fair-to-middlin' player. He tied for second in the 1899 U.S. Open, and from 1900 through 1915 had nine finishes in the top fifteen in the national championship.

Is it possible, then, that George, Jr., gets by to some extent as a representative of golf's earliest American days—that some people feel he must be cared for and preserved, like buildings designated national treasures? Perhaps, because those who barter with George are usually from golf's older establishment and look after the game's traditions, such as Leo Fraser, a former PGA president and owner of the Atlantic City Country Club, which dates back to the turn of the century and is Low's summer headquarters.

Never mind that Low has no more of a Scots brogue than a Broadway bookmaker. After all, he was born in New Jersey (on July 5, 1912). But, of course, George was not chary about acting out his heritage, if the price was right. At George S. May's high-rolling, colorful pro-tour extravaganzas of the 1950s at Chicago's Tam O' Shanter Country Club, the promoter brought in an Egyptian pro who played in a fez, Joe Louis was entered in the amateur field "on his boxing record," and May paid another golfer to play in kilts, argyle knee-socks, and a tam-o'-shanter. That last character was played by our George Low.

Another aspect of Low's draw has a seemingly contradictory slant. He is, on average, quite blunt and direct—honest, really, at least by his lights. That is a rare commodity in our day of the public relations smile and the bland-soup, noncommittal remark. Besides, Low pulls off his put-downs with a nicely honed wit. Once, at a tour event, a pro known for his lax credit rating asked Low for a loan of fifty dollars. George gave a grunt and said, "That's like sending lettuce by rabbit."

But in the end, perhaps the most compelling reason for the care and feeding of George Low is that he has demonstrated beyond all doubt, and over a long period of time, that he owns a very special talent: one that most golfers do not possess and would give up much to acquire, even for a day, just to see what it is like. George Low can *putt*. Truly putt. This is the stuff of unquestioned respect and admiration, not to say envy. The man can see the *line*, and he can put his ball on it at the correct *speed*. Time and time again.

That sounds so simple, and for George it apparently is. I have seen a lot of golfers perform in my thirty-seven years around the game, including all the great putters of the time—Bobby Locke, Billy Casper, Jack Nicklaus, Ben Crenshaw, Tom Watson. But I have never seen anyone in the putting position who looks so surely in place, who so obviously belongs where he is, as does George Low. Low stands on his throne more confidently than any tsar ever sat on his.

Indeed, I found it difficult to get George to demonstrate some of the poor putting positions and strokes he discusses in this book. In this there was some of his natural obstinacy and crankiness, but asking him to misalign his body and the clubhead was like telling the Rock of Gibraltar to face a bit more west. Which reminds me of the most significant thing I have personally gotten from this book (coming upon it before finding the Arnold Palmer remark quoted earlier). That is, to *stand still* when making the putting stroke, not to let the body *move*, especially on shorter putts, when movement is practically imperceptible but can terribly damage the direction of the club.

I should mention that the ideas George Low propounds in this book are not the way many of the game's best players are trying to putt these days. Thus, George is strictly in character by not giving in to the current fashion in putting. This I believe is the mark of a man who has total faith in his method, who believes he is *right,* now and forever. Since he has been "going good" his way for over fifty years, who can deny him?

Finally, in collaborating on this book I feel I have achieved something of a coup. George Low has long been famous for his secrecy, particularly in respect to his putting method. Thus, on that day at the 1982 Tournament Players Championship, in Jacksonville, when George stopped me and said, in his crisp and straightforward style, "Let's do a book on putting," I felt two things. First, I had somehow captured the trust of the cautious old master. Two, I had a scoop.

Al Barkow
Upper Montclair, N.J.
September 1982

THE MASTER OF PUTTING

There are those who like to say that putting is a different game than golf, that it is rolling a ball along the ground whereas golf is hitting a ball through the air. The distinction is obvious, but it doesn't make for different games. In my opinion, the people who talk most about putting and golf being different, and maintain that the two shouldn't be mixed, are lousy putters looking for an excuse or alibi. It won't wash, in my book.

First of all, the closer you get to the hole the less force you need to propel the ball into the cup. Unless the game is radically changed to eliminate putting—let's say by giving so many points for hitting a drive into the fairway, so many points for hitting an iron shot to within a certain distance of the pin—you are always going to have to make a smaller, milder stroke to finish a hole. So why not just accept it! Besides, even when hitting the ball through the air, you must allow for a certain amount of roll along the ground once it comes down.

What's more, the putting stroke and the swing with the other clubs are basically the same operation. One strike is simply longer than the other, and takes the use of the bigger muscles. How many times have you experimented with your full swing and found a piece of business you could adapt to your putting stroke (and vice versa), such as completing the follow-through, or slowing down the backswing? Except for the shortest of putts, a good backswing with a driver or iron is the same as with the putter, to the inside of the target line. And at impact you want the clubface square to the target, be it driver or putter.

I am well aware that putting is the most individualistic, even idiosyncratic, part of golf. There have been a lot of different stances, grips, and strokes among the best golfers to play the game. Yet, there is a common thread running through the methods of all good putters. I will point them out as we go along.

To putt well takes patience, study, care, and, in my mind, a lot more cunning and sheer nerve than it takes to haul off and hit a ball as hard as you can with the longer clubs. Speaking of cunning, I remember some of the old-time pros would spit on their ball when they had a fast downhill putt, to keep it from going too far. Golf had its "spitter," and only Ky Laffoon couldn't use it. He chewed tobacco, so if he spat on his ball the officials would see it.

Anyway, if all you want out of the game is to hit the ball as hard as you can, then you may as well play all your golf at a driving range—and you could sure call *that* a different game.

Figuring two putts per green as par for the putting part of the game means you should take thirty-six putts per round. No touring pro could expect to make any kind of living out there at that rate. Even an average of thirty-one or thirty-two putts a round is not going to cut it these days—which is the best indicator I know of how important putting is. For the average golfer this is no less true. Take even thirty-six putts a round, and you are practically guaranteed of breaking one hundred every time out. One way or another, for players of all levels of ability, almost half the strokes used in a round of golf are on the greens.

Yet, despite all the obvious points showing how important putting is, the majority of players—good and bad—do very little about trying to improve this part of their game. Many of these people are the ones who complain that putting is not golf. Most say they just flat out can't putt, or that putting is a mystery. At the same time, they spend very little time on the practice putting clock; usually at most they casually hit a few putts just before teeing off for a round. Also, teaching pros are rarely asked for putting lessons. Everyone wants to figure out how to hit a high draw with a driver, or how not to slice, which is okay, but few will bother to educate themselves in making ten-foot putts, even though they know this ability can make up for many a poor drive or approach shot.

I can understand that it is probably more exciting to hit a big drive than to roll a ball along the ground. When the good drive comes off, there is a terrific sensation and feeling of satisfaction at having successfully brought together so many different working parts. There is also the expression of strength, power, which is good for the ego. Putting can't really compare with hitting the big shots, in this respect. There is no turf flying, no whoosh of air, no ball soaring through the sky. Nevertheless, I've seen and heard a lot of joyful jumping and whooping, a lot of laughter and celebration, when a curling twenty-footer rolls into the hole.

In any case, it has always been my impression that all golfers play mainly to make a good score, and also to make a better score than the guys they are playing with. The golfer who makes the best score has *always* done some very good putting. There are a lot of fellows working in pro shops who can hit shots as good as a Nicklaus or a Watson, but who never figured out a way to get the ball in the hole.

It's not something I prefer to dwell on, but I suppose it's true some people have a natural gift for putting— that somehow they have been given a fine sense of touch for stroking the ball at the right speed, for "seeing" the line, and so on. Such people are, of course, very fortunate, but even they must put some time in regularly concentrating on and practicing their gift if they are going to get full advantage from it. I think I was given a special ability to putt—I have always been good at things that take touch, such as bowling, billiards, and so forth—but I *know* I cultivated my gift with many, many hours of practice on the putting clock at Carnoustie when I was a young man.

As for the less gifted, which may or may not be the majority (it is hard to tell where a gift leaves off and hard work takes over to bring putting success), I am convinced they can become good putters who will not destroy every round with three-putt greens and misses from in close. They might even become *very* good putters, at least on occasion. Take Leo Diegel, for example, who was so great a shotmaker in the 1930s he could give such contemporaries as Jimmy Thomson and Craig Wood a stroke a side in practice rounds and beat them. Poor putting plagued Diegel throughout most of his career, especially in tournament competition. Eventually, he developed a strange-looking, elbows-akimbo putting style in an effort to beat his nerves and lack of confidence about putting. With this, Leo managed to

win two PGA championships in a row, plus other tour-
naments against men like Walter Hagen and Gene Sara-
zen.

Joe Turnesa, one of a famous family of top-notch golfers, was a terrible putter most of his career, but he kept
on trying—and would try anything. He once won the
Long Island Open, a tour-level event in his day, using a
putter that was less than two feet long.

The side-saddle technique Sam Snead adopted in the
latter years of his career is another example of the point
I'm trying to make: that even the worst of putters
should never give up hope, or stop trying to find ways to
improve. There *is* a way to putt better, a *technique*. It is
not a mystery. I think I will help you with my ideas in
this book but you will help yourself as much if not more
by simply working at the art of putting. Think about it
when you're not on the course, concentrate on it when
you are, and practice, practice, *practice*.

There is absolutely nothing more frustrating than to
hit two fine shots—a great drive and a crisp iron onto a
green—then three-putt. Or to hit an approach stiff to
the pin, then miss the birdie putt. I have heard many
golfers complain that this kind of thing takes a lot of the
fun out of the game. I agree. The solution is to make
good putting as much fun as hitting good full shots. If I
can get you into this frame of mind with this book, get
you more interested in putting, I will feel I have really
helped you, even if you don't use the mechanics I recommend.

It just so happens that shotmaking comes first in golf,
followed by putting. Thus, given the nature of things,
when a golfer hits a very good shot onto a green he
sometimes, in the bliss of that achievement, will fail to
complete the work with a good, well-thought-out putt.

It is as though the real work were done with the approach shot, and the rest were only child's play. Some golfers will admit they feel putting is insignificant after having hit great shots to the green, and thus will not pay much attention to completing the job. Or, with an easy par assured, they will be overcautious or precise on the birdie putt. These are some of the reasons why many golfers hit those "exploders," putts of only fifteen or twenty feet that run five or six feet past the cup as if they were shot from a gun. That happens when the mind leaves the body, when you go into a coma and don't think properly about what you are doing or are supposed to do with the putter.

As I have already suggested, putting is not as sensational as hitting full shots, and consequently not as interesting, so golfers are apt to slump off at it. Also, putting has a much smaller margin for error, is a more painstaking business. Many people just do not like to deal with such fine-tuning because it is nervous-making, maybe even a little scary—especially since they know in their hearts how important putting is to the overall success of their game. Bringing these two central aspects of golf together—hitting and putting—is primarily a psychological problem, but it does have a mechanical side to it. Very often, if you come up with some mechanics in which you can believe, and that seem to work more often than not, the psychological side of the issue just fades away.

You have to remember there are two different movements in golf: you hit full shots hard, with force and, therefore, a lot of body action; but when you putt, your body must be very quiet, very still. The only parts that move are the arms *from the elbows down*. Between the time when you have hit the ball onto the green and you stroke it with a putter, you must change your thinking cap—go from force to finesse. To me, this makes the game all the more interesting to play. Golf would get very boring if all you did was bang out one shot after another with woods and irons, just as it would get boring if all you did was hit putts.

What one person finds boring, another might find fascinating. Personality plays no small role in putting, both in the interest one takes in it and the style one employs. Generally speaking, someone who tends to be quick-thinking, quick-talking, quick-moving is going to be an aggressive putter, banging the ball against the back of the cup. I don't believe this type of personality is as effective a putter, in the long run, as the type who goes about life in a more relaxed, less intense way. Fast swingers of golf clubs, such as Lanny Wadkins, tend to play well only in spurts and have a shorter life span at the top of their game than the slower-swinging, casual Julius Boros–type golfer.

There is only one thing you can do about this situation if you are a fast-paced person: realize it, accept it, adapt your game to it, and hope for the best. Speed does not always kill. Doug Ford has always played rapidly and putted quickly but has had a very fine and long career. Tom Watson is another upbeat swinger/putter who is doing pretty nicely. If either tried to go against his personality he probably would never be able to get the club back.

However, if you feel you can slow down without hurting your game, if you feel it will bring an improvement, do it and then *work* at it. A good example of this has been Don January, who admitted he was a hot-tempered, fast-footed fellow and that he made a very conscious effort early in his career to do everything more slowly and to never lose his cool. The result has been an extended career at the top of the game.

Am I saying that slow is better than fast, in putting if not all of golf playing? Yes, I am, and I will stick with that. In my experience, the best putters have almost invariably been slow movers. Walter Hagen took five minutes to reach for and lift a salt shaker, forty-five minutes to shave. He just *never* rushed into anything. Bobby Jones had an even-paced fluidity to his game, and Jack Nicklaus has always played—and in particular putted— with a very deliberate, slow-tempo action. On the other hand, I think of Ben Hogan, who had a very fast-paced golf swing and a terrible case of the putting yips at the end of his career. Arnold Palmer was always a very aggressive, very fast swinger of the club, and he lost his once-great putting touch while still pretty much in his prime of life as a golfer.

Speaking of aggressiveness, I want right at the outset to make clear my position on the "never up, never in" idea. I think it is absolutely right. Bobby Jones once said something about knowing for sure that a putt past the hole did not go in, and people have interpreted that to mean Jones thought it was better being an inch or so short of the cup, leaving a simple tap-in, rather than a couple of feet past, leaving a touchy "come-backer" to make. In fact, Jones advocated hitting putts that died around the cup so they had a chance of falling in at any of the edges, instead of skidding by if hit too strongly. I can accept the idea of not wanting the pressure of a two- or three-footer coming back to the hole every time, but the golfer is rare who has the touch to have his putts die at the hole every time. Therefore, as far as I am concerned, I would rather err on the long side. What's the good of hitting a putt right on line that comes up short? Nothing. Indeed, I recommend visualizing the hole a foot farther away than it actually is as a way of making sure you get the ball all the way to the cup.

As I conclude this introduction I come down to my two basic tenets of putting, mechanics aside—tempo and practice. These two words will run through most of everything I will say about grip, stance, stroke, and so forth. Good putting results from *repetition*, doing the same thing with the blade every time, and a repeating stroke comes from tempo and practice, practice and tempo. That may not sound very precise, but putting is not an exact science—and it does not hurt to understand that, too.

For instance, there is a device to measure the speed of greens called the Stimpmeter. It's an inclined chute through which balls are rolled onto greens. Every ball comes out of the chute at the same speed and on the same line—there is no human-error factor. You would think, under this circumstance, with the chute aimed at a hole six or seven feet away, that every ball rolled out would go in the hole. That doesn't happen. Sometimes the ball does not go in. No one can explain why it misses, and I doubt if anyone will ever be able to.

In other words, you are a fool to blame yourself for every putt that does not fall, and particularly those you are sure you hit as right as could be. Some things, sometimes, are simply out of our control. At the same time, you would be foolish not to find a way to hit as many putts "as right as could be," because, as a gambling man, I can tell you that you will then be giving yourself the best odds for success, for overcoming the fate factor.

CHAPTER 1

THE GRIP

DON'T PRESSURE IT

The first thing to remember about the mechanics of putting is that this part of the game does not require physical strength. Because of that, you do not have to grip the putter tightly.

Many golfers grip the club too tightly when hitting full shots, and that's understandable because a great deal of pressure is being exerted on the hands. Much less pressure is required for the putting stroke, so an over-tight grip not only desensitizes your hands—more particularly, your fingers—but almost always leads to a short, quick backstroke. A short, quick backstroke is a yip stroke, now or in future. A short, quick stroke makes it very difficult to hit putts at the correct speed every time.

In general, you want a *light* hold on the club for putting. Now, how light is light? That is hard for me, or anyone else, to say, because each of you have your own sense of what is secure, loose, tight. As a general rule, though, you are holding the putter too tightly if a lot of putts are going to the right of your target, or you are

*Too tight — reject
tar loose — com up short
+ the left*

The Grip   13

hitting a lot of exploders. Conversely, you are holding the club too loosely if your putts are consistently coming up short and/or to the left of the hole.

A good way to find the proper grip pressure while over the ball is to squeeze and unsqueeze the handle a number of times, until you come to the pressure that is most comfortable.

THE FINGERS HAVE IT

The palms of the hands have little sensitivity, at least for the purpose of putting, so it is counterproductive to hold the club with them. Therefore, the first rule in adopting a putting grip, before considering any other facet, is to hold as much of the club as possible in the fingers of both hands. I can go even further on this. If some sort of tragic accident happened to me and I had to choose which fingers I wanted left on my hands, I would go for the thumb and forefinger of the right hand, and the thumb of the left hand, in that order of preference.

When you put your hand in your pocket to get a coin, you do not find the item with your palm, or even the second, third, and fourth fingers. You separate the coin from others, then clutch it and lift it with the thumb and forefinger. These same digits provide the greatest control of the putter, plus the greatest sense of touch needed for good putting. In this regard, think of putting as the work of a pickpocket, with the grip designed to get the job done.

Furthermore, at those times when you must increase the grip pressure—when putting on very slow or wet greens, or when going uphill and/or into heavy grain—

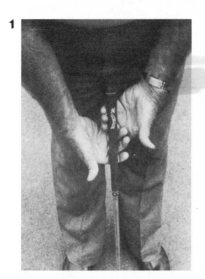

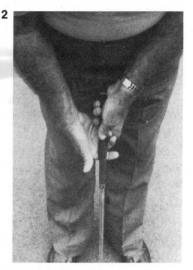

Grip Club in Fingers. The palms of the hands offer little sensitivity for putting, so the club should not be centered in them. The club is held in the last three fingers of the left hand and first three fingers of the right hand in the initial stage of setting the grip. (ILLUSTRATION #1)   As the hands close, the thumb of the left hand is shortened and set firmly on the center of the handle. (ILLUSTRATION #2)   When the right hand closes, its thumb is also centered firmly on the handle. (ILLUSTRATION #3)   The most pressure—the *real gripping*—is exerted by the thumbs and right forefinger (ILLUSTRATION #4), the latter positioned as in triggering a gun. In the final position, the back of the left hand faces directly in the opposite direction. (ILLUSTRATION #3).

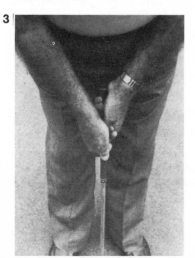

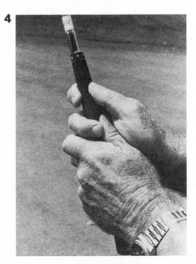

press *only* the thumbs and the right forefinger into the handle a bit more than you would normally.

THE FINGER ARRANGEMENT

As for the arrangement of the hands and fingers on the club handle, there are a few different putting grips that have been developed over the years, with variations on them, plus a few oddball types.

The most common putting grip is the reverse Vardon overlap, in which the left index finger is nested in the crease between the first two fingers of the right hand. Variations of this include the first two fingers of the left hand, or the left index finger only, laying down across the knuckles of the right hand. Then there is the interlocking grip, the index finger of the left hand intertwined with the pinky of the right hand. Another way to hold the putter is with the full-fingered grip, also called the baseball grip, wherein the fingers of both hands wrap around the handle, except for the thumbs, which usually lie down the center of the club.

Among the more radical departures from the standard putting grip is the cross-handed technique, wherein the left hand is placed below the right and the left pinky overlaps the crease between the first two fingers of the right hand. Then there's the split-hand grip Phil Rodgers tried once on the tour after getting it from Paul Runyan. Here the left hand is at the top of the club handle, with the right set about ten inches below, on the shaft itself.

Of course, there is the standard Vardon overlap—the right index finger overlapping the crease between the first and second fingers of the left hand. Because this is the way most golfers hold the club to hit full shots, there are those who say it is best for putting, too, because you then have consistency for all shots. However, the standard Vardon overlap is not used very much, nor recommended by many experts, because it can work counter to a fundamental element in the putting stroke, the action of the left hand.

Inaction of the left hand would probably be a better word, because the biggest single problem in putting is the left hand breaking down in the forward stroke. By "breaking down" I mean a cocking forward of the left hand or wrist on the through-stroke, which almost always causes putts to be pulled left of the target. With the standard Vardon overlap (and also the "baseball" grip) the left hand is vulnerable to breaking down, which is precisely why the Vardon overlap is used in full shotmaking, where you want and need some left-hand flexibility to get power. The cross-handed grip is actually the ultimate guard against left-hand breakdown, but seems to prevent a fine touch for longer putts. It's good for the shorter ones, but over fifteen feet the tendency is to hit the ball too hard.

The interlocking grip is a good guard against left-hand breakdown, which is probably why Nicklaus uses it. So is the reverse Vardon overlap, which puts one more finger of the right hand on the handle—the pinky—and so may offer a little more touch.

MY GRIP

My own grip is a variation on the reverse Vardon overlap. Instead of the left index finger sitting in the crease

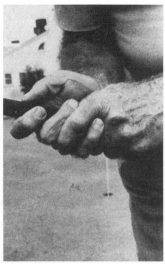

The Low Version of the Reverse Overlap.
 The index finger of the left hand rides on top of the third finger of the right hand, and the pinky finger of the right hand lays against this combination. There is no actual interlocking, but the same kind of solidity is achieved.

between the pinky and third finger of the right hand, it rides directly on top of the third finger. This leaves the right pinky loose and free, and it is simply placed against the wall formed by the overriding index finger. Finally, there is a gap between my right thumb and forefinger, with the forefinger positioned as in triggering a gun. I have heard suggestions that the right thumb and forefinger should touch, but this would reduce the amount of feel obtained through the tips of these digits resting on the club handle.

 I like my grip because it brings the hands as close to- gether as possible, and setting the hands close together makes for better putting (and all shotmaking generally). This is another reason why the split-hand grip is especially bad. Another advantage of my grip is that it makes it easier to keep the thumbs centered on the handle. This to me is a very important part of the grip: both thumbs should always be flush on the handle. In fact, I go as far as to dig the tips of my thumbs into the grip, but that's just a personal habit. So long as the tips of the right index finger are in solid, flush contact with the putter handle, you will get maximum feel and club control.

To be honest, any of the reverse Vardon overlap grips, or the interlocking grip, will bring the hands close together, and thereby make it easier to keep the thumbs centered on the handle. However, my version best facilitates the kind of putting stroke I advocate.

GIVE IT THE BACK OF YOUR HANDS

There is one more basic in the positioning of the hands on the club. To recap first, you hold the club in the fingers, with special emphasis on the thumbs and right index finger; the thumbs lie down the center of the handle; you use some version of the reverse Vardon overlap. Finally, you set the hands so that *the back of the left directly faces the target and the back of the right faces directly away from the target.*

In this respect, the position of the left hand is especially important. When you look down at your left hand, you should never see any knuckles. Oddly, in golf terminology this is known as a "weak" grip, even though it is meant to prevent the left hand from breaking down. (It is weak in that it makes for less flexible wrist action, which is why many touring pros use it for their full shots. Their hand action is so powerful that if they used the "strong" left hand the average golfer generally uses, and should, with the hand turned to the right so that at least two knuckles show, the pros would hook their shots very badly.)

As for the right hand, you could turn it so far to the right that its back faces the ground and you would not be doing a bad thing. Anything in this direction is better than the reverse, the right hand turned to the left, because this alignment is likely to set your right shoulder too far forward, and also make the right hand play too strong a part in the forward stroke.

Turn Right hand the other way

LEFT IS RUDDER, RIGHT IS DRIVE SHAFT

Behind all this discussion of the grip is a central concept. You might liken it to sailing. The left hand is the rudder that keeps the ship (putter) "steady as she goes," while the right hand is the drive shaft providing propulsion, direction, and the touch for speed.

EVERY SHOT AT THE SAME STATION

One last thing about the grip, although this also relates to the stroke. I hold the putter at the very end or top of the handle *for putts of all lengths.* A lot of golfers like to choke down for short putts, but this changes the swing-weight of the club and can cause your basic stroke and touch to change. Wherever you like to hold the club, stay at that station for every putt you play.

CHAPTER 2

THE STANCE

ROCK-STEADY, ON-LINE COMFORT

In taking your position at the ball there are three primary considerations. First, you must be comfortable. Second, you must be properly aligned to your target. Third, you must set up in a way that allows you to avoid any body movement during the stroke.

I cannot tell an individual what will make him comfortable, nor even tell by looking at him if he is or isn't comfortable. I will say this, however: you can get into an address position that may *feel* comfortable but is not actually conducive to good putting. So, although some of the suggestions I make about the stance may seem uncomfortable at first, give them a fair try. That way you may eventually get used to them, and thereby feel at ease.

Everything about the putting stance I recommend is simple and natural in form, because it's based on flexibility at the joints, plus relaxed muscles. Just as you will never see a good dancer dancing stiff-legged, so you will never see a good putter with legs rigid or stiff at the knees, or with arms taut and stressed. Everyone bends some at the waist when putting, because that's pretty hard to avoid with so short a club. However, I believe it's better to bend almost into a crouch than to "stand tall," because by standing too upright at the ball you are liable to lose flex in your knees, which makes for instability. Set up too tall, and you also end up with the putter relatively upright, and the tendency then is to swing the club back to the outside of the target line.

I also recommend that the elbows be kept close to the body, because that's the natural way for them to hang. By doing this you further avoid stiffness, which is always the sense you get when you see golfers putting with their elbows sticking out. The right elbow will stick out a little, which is natural, but you don't want to exaggerate it for fear of opening or closing the clubface during the stroke. What is more, by keeping the elbows close to your body, and always slightly flexed, you give yourself a far better chance of not moving your shoulders during the stroke.

Alignment, as it is conventionally defined, pretty much begins and ends for me with the setting of the clubface square to the line of putt. I say this because I believe everyone should putt with a slightly open stance: that is, the left foot drawn back a little from the target line. I take the same open stance for all putts, from level ones to breaking side-hillers, the only difference being my overall body position in relation to the target line.

Conventional alignment requires the feet, hips, and shoulders to parallel the target line. With the open stance, of course, the feet, hips, and shoulders are aimed left of the target line.

The Basic Address Position. The weight is concentrated on the left heel, the knees are slightly flexed, there is some bend at the waist. Elbows are close in to the body and the arms hang naturally with a slight flex. The hands are also very close to the body.

The clubface is set facing the target line (in this picture slightly left of the cup). The stance itself is open, with the left foot drawn a little back from the target line.

The ball is played inside the left heel, and far enough from the feet so that the putter is at approximately a forty-five-degree angle to the body. The feet are set fairly close together, about the same distance as the width of the shoulders. The hands are slightly ahead of the ball, which promotes the slightly descending blow.

Elbows Out. An exaggerated demonstration of what can happen when putting with the elbows away from the body, one elbow pointing directly toward and the other away from the target line. You are apt to shut the blade on the backstroke, and, in compensating, open it wide at impact. Misdirection is practically guaranteed. Elbows in this position also encourage—in fact, pretty much necessitate—some upper-body, and especially shoulder, movement.

WHY THE OPEN STANCE IS BETTER

With an open stance you get a better visual sense of the target—more frontal rather than, in the square alignment, kind of peeking around the corner and getting a distorted view of your goal. The open stance also allows the hands (and, therefore, the putter) to flow easily forward in the downstroke, because they are not blocked by the left side. Finally, the open stance also makes it easier to keep the right shoulder low and behind the ball, Jack Nicklaus being a perfect example of this among present-day top players.

The Closed Stance. An exaggerated demonstration of what must be done to make a closed stance work. The right shoulder will—must—go forward or "over the top" in order to get the blade moving down the *true* target line at impact. This is a risky business in terms of consistency.

ANYTHING BUT CLOSED

I am saying the stance should be *slightly* open, but you can open it as much as you like and still be all right. You can also stand square to your target if you prefer, but this makes you susceptible to a closed position, with the feet, hips, shoulders, *and* the putter blade aiming to the right of your target. When you set up closed the natural tendency is to bring the right shoulder outward, or "over the top," in the downstroke in order to get the putter blade moving directly along the target line. You may get the blade on line once in a while, but over the long haul this is an unsound and unsafe method of putting. In fact, the only good putter I have ever seen who putted from a closed stance was Bobby Locke. One out of thousands is not a percentage that breeds confidence.

STANDING FIRM

On the matter of body movement, I leave no room for individual tastes. *To avoid movement you must concentrate your weight on your left heel.* You don't have to exaggerate to a point where you look like the Leaning Tower of Pisa, but your weight must be there—predominantly on the left heel.

Setting the weight back on *both* heels also provides good stability, but by doing this you risk getting too far away from the ball. No matter how you stand—open, closed, crouched, upright, or whatever—*your eyes must be directly over the ball.*

With your weight mostly on the right foot, the tendency is to shift your body to the left with the swing of the putter during the forward stroke, or to stay back on the right side and pull the ball to the left. Setting the weight on the toes is the worst of all. Then you can rarely be well balanced, and will be leaning forward to where your eyes are, out beyond the ball at address, so that you're more or less looking back at it—the worst kind of distortion. And, of course, you're very likely to move during the stroke because of your discomfort.

So, putt with your weight predominantly on your left heel. Set up thus, and you will find it difficult to move your body in any direction during the stroke.

What happens when you pull the putter to the left. Aug 25-2019

PLAYING BETWEEN YOUR FEET

There are other important considerations in setting up
to putt. One of them is the position of the ball in relation to your feet. Here again I am unequivocal. The ball
must be played somewhere between your heels. You can
have it off the left heel, or farther back toward the middle of your feet if that suits you. *Never should the ball be
forward off your left heel.*

Many golfers play the ball forward of their left
heel—usually off the left toe—under the mistaken notion that they want to contact it on the upstroke, with
the blade on the rise. Positioning the ball forward promotes this all right, but consistently solid ball contact is
far less likely, first, because you are subject to having the
putter face open or shut at impact and, second, because
you encourage body movement during the stroke.

Because repetition in all aspects of putting is critical
to success, you should play the ball in the same position

every time, for *every kind of putt*—straight, breaking downhill, uphill. However, on putts of thirty feet or more, and especially on slow greens or going uphill, it is a good idea to move the ball a bit more toward the middle of your feet. Playing the longer putts forward of the left heel is especially risky, not only because you are asking for poor direction, but also because you are not going to get the kind of hit, *naturally,* that you need to cover the distance. When the ball's too far forward, instinct tells you to hit it harder, and this results in forced hand action, which usually causes putter-face misdirection, and body movement.

With the ball set inside the left heel (or even farther back toward the middle of your feet), you can also easily set your hand slightly ahead of it at address, which is another fundamental of fine putting.

DISTANCE FROM THE BALL

How far should you stand from the ball in the putting stance? The answer depends on whether you set up flat or upright. I think a flat position is better: that is, the hands set relatively low, with the putter held out to the ball so that the shaft is at about a forty-five-degree angle from the body. In this case, you will stand fairly well away from the ball. If you prefer an upright position, with the putter shaft angled at around eighty degrees, you will naturally stand closer to the ball. However, in my view, the upright position makes it difficult to swing the club back to the inside. Also, you are apt to close or hood the blade on the backstroke. I'll talk more about these two factors in the chapter on the stroke.

I have seen very few outstanding putters who were upright at address, whereas there have been many who take the flatter mode. Isao Aoki is a prime example of the flat position, although he does somewhat exaggerate it.

In either case, the distance you stand from the ball at address is determined by the angling of the club shaft. The flatter you position it, the farther from the ball you should be, given that you're using a putter of standard length.

WIDTH OF STANCE

I recommend that the feet be separated in the stance no more than your shoulder width, or even closer together if you can manage it. The closer together the feet, the easier it is to concentrate the weight on the left heel.

There are golfers who putt very well with their feet spread very wide apart, their aim in doing so being to gain stability. A wide stance does help keep the body from moving, but it also encourages the use of the shoulders in the stroke, and this is contrary to consistently good putting. Furthermore, over the history of the game there have been no really great putters—no lasting champions—who have spread their feet wide. Among the narrow-stance champions I can name Walter Hagen, Bobby Jones, Lloyd Mangrum, Jack Nicklaus, and Tom Watson. As an old horseplayer I believe in past performance charts, and those guys all get a Triple A rating.

STEPPING UP TO IT—
THE VALUE OF A ROUTINE

You now know all the details of the stance in my system, all the positions I think you should be in when over the ball. Of course, you're not going to think about all those details every time you putt. This is the stuff you practice one or maybe two at a time, to develop memory so that you fall into them automatically when putting for real.

Nevertheless, you should find a routine for getting up to the ball, a consistent pattern of movements. You'll be surprised at how much this contributes to consistency in the way you stroke the ball. On those days when the putter doesn't feel quite right in your hands, a consistent routine for getting into the putt can remind you of the times when you *did* feel right. In a pressure situation, that sort of routine serves as a kind of security blanket—something to count on to get properly organized in the clutch.

THE REHEARSAL

My own pattern of stepping up to putt is nothing special, but every part of it is purposeful. I start from directly behind the ball to get a good perspective on the line of the putt. As I move up beside the ball, I give myself a full dress rehearsal of the stroke. The club is put down beside the ball with the toe almost touching it. The blade is set facing the intended line of putt. My feet and body are arranged as for the putt itself. Finally, I take a practice stroke *at the exact tempo I plan to use for the putt.*

A lot of golfers wonder why the club should be so close to the ball for the rehearsal stroke. They think this risks hitting the ball accidentally and incurring a penalty. Well, it's very, very unusual in my experience for anyone to hit the ball with the practice stroke, because we're talking about a very mild, highly controlled motion. Against the risk there is the advantage that you are simulating *precisely* the positions and stroke you will use for real just a moment later. After the rehearsal stroke, you simply slide the club in behind the ball, move your feet forward a tiny bit, then stroke the putt.

12

13

Stepping in and Rehearsing. Moving in to every putt should be a patterned, repetitious routine because this encourages consistency in the stroke itself.

Start from behind the ball to get a good perspective on the contour and line of the putt, walk to the ball from this position. (ILLUSTRATIONS #12, 13). (*continued on following page*)

Once at the ball, set up only a few inches from it with everything in exactly the same position you will use for the putt itself—face alignment, stance, posture, and so forth. Then take a practice stroke or two at the same tempo you intend to use for the actual putt. (ILLUSTRATIONS #14, 15, 16).

Move slightly forward to address the ball, then stroke it. (ILLUSTRATIONS #17, 18).

GET IT IN THE NECK

Here are a couple more tips.

First, when you put the putter behind the ball don't press it too firmly into the ground. Hold the putter so the blade just touches the grass. Pressing or leaning on the putter at address reduces your feel. Although you are holding the putter firmly there must still be a little give, a little softness in your hands, when you hit the ball, and in pressing the club into the ground the tendency is to grab the club too tightly.

Second, I like to begin to putt with the ball set opposite the back half of the blade—toward the heel, or neck. Clubmakers who put a line or other mark on their putters to indicate the "sweet spot," the most solid part of a putter head, usually put them in the center of the blade. That is not necessarily the location of the sweet

The Stroke Up Close. The ball is set near the neck of the putter, which assures hitting it with the most solid portion of the clubhead and also promotes swinging back to the inside of the target line.

The putt in this picture breaks from right to left, but the blade is aimed and the stroke is made as if it were a straight putt . . . to the right of the cup.

spot (as I'll discuss in the chapter on equipment); thus I believe it is safer, and more of a guarantee you'll hit the ball with the most solid part of the head, to set the ball toward the neck. (On center-shafted putters, set the ball opposite the point where the shaft joins the head.)

This position also has a way of assuring that the back-stroke will be to the inside of the target line. Why I think the club should take this path is covered in the next chapter.

CHAPTER 3

THE STROKE

ON THE DOWNBEAT

I won't beat around the bush about the putting stroke I use, and believe is the best. The key feature is striking the ball with a slightly *descending* putter head—on the downbeat, as I like to say.

This is the opposite of what many people think, or are told to think, is the best way to putt: to hit the ball with a slightly ascending putter head—on the upbeat. The theory here is that an ascending strike imparts overspin to the ball, giving it a better roll. Conversely, therefore, people assume that a putter head hitting a ball on the downbeat will impart underspin, or that hitting the ball on a dead-level plane will put no spin on it at all.

The scientific fact is that *no* effective spin is imparted to a putted ball, no matter at what angle the putter strikes it. The ball first skids or slides along the ground for a short distance, then begins to roll. In terms of physics, the angle of the putter head contributes nothing to that rolling action, which always takes the form of overspin. The ratio of skid is generally about twenty percent of the full length of a putt.

A Side View of the Stroke. The body is very "quiet" throughout; the only movement is from the elbows down.

The wrists break to some extent, but this action could hardly be considered flippy, especially as at impact the hands are in exactly the same position they were in at address.

The ball is hit with a slightly descending blow, and the short follow-through has the club stopping while still in or on the ground for a putt of about ten feet.

However, it has also been shown scientifically that a ball can be made to roll sooner after the impact *if it is struck above its center.* Now, with my downbeat stroke—assuming the putter blade is of standard depth—the top half of the face will strike the ball *just above its center,* which means the ball gets into over-spin—or true roll—almost as soon as it is struck.

The angle of descent (and ascent) of my stroke is about that of a very shallow saucer—the putter head is not coming down off a cliff to hit the ball. This produces a more positive, more emphatic blow than a rising hit, and those qualities are obtained without any artificial manipulation by the golfer. It is in the nature of a descending blow—be it with a hammer, a guillotine, a putter—to be, not only more solid, more forceful, but more controlled: the putter head is not apt to change alignment at the crucial moment when it meets the ball.

Think of it this way: when you paint a flat surface going from top to bottom, you are emulating a putting stroke. Your best work is done—the most paint gets on with the least effort—with the first touch of the brush, which comes from a downward stroke. On the upward part of the sweep there is a thinner application of paint. In short, the descending putting stroke at impact is the most efficient and effective.

FROM THE INSIDE

There is a second important aspect to the path of the stroke—its angle in relation to the target line. As I suggested at the end of the previous chapter, that angle

A Rear View of the Stroke. The eyes are directly over the ball at address, and the open stance allows the best look at the line of putt. The open stance also lets the club move freely down that line, after impact.

The backstroke is to the inside of the line of putt, and for a putt of this length—about twenty feet—the club is raised fairly high off the ground. After the descending blow the blade rises up only a little on the follow-through.

There has been no upper-arm or shoulder movement, and the rest of the body is also very still throughout the stroke.

should always be to the inside of the target line on the backstroke, with a return to square along the target line at impact. Actually, the full shape of a good putting stroke is a shallow crescent, with the follow-through the same length as the backstroke.

What's wrong with a straight-back, straight-through putting stroke? Nothing—for putts under two feet. Above that distance, there's nothing wrong with it *if you can do it.* Unfortunately, that's tough, if only because it is an unnatural motion. A backstroke a foot long or longer will of its own accord want to go inside the target line, just as the club in a full golf swing will do so once it gets more than a few feet from the ball. To keep the clubhead from swinging inside requires manipulation by the golfer, and the golfer who manipulates the club is setting himself up to err.

The most common tendency with a straight stroke is to take the club to the outside of the target line on the backswing. When you swing back on the same path, you will cut across the ball and pull it to the left of your target—although you could also push it to the right if the face is open. This is the classic slicer's action in full-swing golf.

The alternative would be to redirect the stroke, swinging it back on the outside, then, before the downstroke begins, working the club back onto the target line or to the inside of it. The dangers in this kind of action should be obvious.

So, the club swings back to the inside pretty much of its own accord—especially if you set up with the hands relatively low, and the ball opposite the back half of the blade, then return to the ball on the same path, squaring to the target at the moment of impact. A good image to picture this action is that of a swinging door: the club is the door, which hangs on and swings around a hinge that is your hands.

WRISTY BUT NOT FLIPPY

As I said, the action of my stroke is comparatively wristy. However, while my wrists do break or cock a little on the backstroke, there is a *firmness* at all times. Mine is not a flippy stroke—loose or uncontrolled—largely because of the pressure exerted on the handle by my thumbs and right forefinger. I believe that not letting the wrists cock would, once again, be unnatural in respect to the path of the backstroke. For the club to go back to the inside, *there has to be some wrist cock.*

I use a slight modification for putts over thirty feet, especially on slow greens. Then the overall action is not strictly from "the elbows down." Some upper arm and shoulder movement becomes necessary in order to achieve the necessary force and yet still maintain proper clubface alignment. The stroke remains wristy, but it is now synchronized with some movement of the upper arms and shoulders.

AN "OPEN" AND "SHUT" CASE?

My right hand—specifically, my right thumb and forefinger—takes the club back and to the inside of the target line. The blade *appears* to open, and it *appears* to close on the forward stroke. Note I say *appears* to open

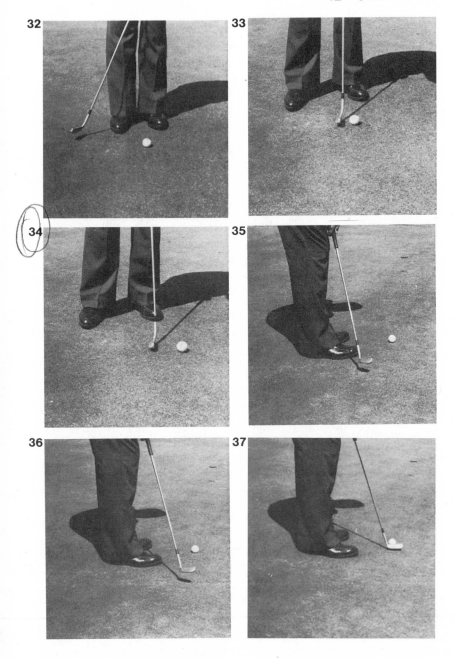

The Swinging Door. While the blade works slightly up and down, and from inside to square, overall the putter also functions like a swinging door. The putter blade seems to open on the backstroke (ILLUSTRATION #32), but in fact remains square to the path of swing—just like an opening door.

Proof of this is that, without any manipulation on my part, the blade returns to the ball in exactly the same square-to-target-line position it was in at address (ILLUSTRATIONS #33, 34).

For further proof that the blade remains square, rather than opening, see the rear view of the backstroke (ILLUSTRATIONS #35, 36, 37). If the blade actually opened on the backstroke, its toe (in ILLUSTRATION #35) would be fanned out and pointing more toward the camera.

Notice in all these pictures that the blade does not hug the ground on the backstroke. This is frequently advocated by putting teachers, but not by me.

By contrast with the square blade, there is the hooded blade (ILLUSTRATION #38) that many mistake for being square. Here the face of the blade faces more directly at the ground. The hooded blade requires an unhooding at impact—an opening up. Compare the blade or face positions in ILLUSTRATIONS #34 and #39; the former is square as at address, the latter has been unhooded, an artificial manipulation that could very well misdirect the ball.

and close. In fact, the putter face remains throughout in a square position *relative to the path on which the club is swinging.* In other words, if the target line could somehow be swung around with the movement of the putter face during the backstroke, as though attached to it, the two would remain in *an unchanging relationship* to each other.

A good way to get the feel of this is to make a putting stroke hitting, let's say, toward the north. Now stop the backstroke about half way, holding the blade in position, then turn your body to face east. If you now put the blade back on the ground you will find it to be square to the target line. If the putter face truly opened, which would require a definite manipulation of the club with the hands, you and an observer would see the toe of the club flare or fan out on the backstroke, then turn back on the forward stroke.

I stress these points because most golfers are accustomed to seeing that the putter face remains square *in relation to a target that remains stationary,* that is, the ball. There is nothing wrong with this in theory, but in practice it involves closing or shutting down the blade relative to the swing path—what we pros usually call "hooding." Most golfers who don't allow some wrist cock in their putting strokes are apt to hood the putter by rotating their left hand counterclockwise—moving it in such a way that its back faces more toward the ground. If you hood the putter going back, the inclination is to unhood or open it through impact—or even to close it yet more as you hit the ball. This either pushes putts to the right, or pulls them left of the target.

There have been a few good putters who have hooded the blade—Billy Casper, Bob Rosburg, and Horton

Smith come to mind in this respect. However, all three were saved by the fact that they hit the ball with a *descending* blow, and thus reduced the risk of opening or shutting the blade at impact.

pull

LOW ON LOW BACKSTROKES

Many golfers have been told that good putting comes from keeping the club low to the ground on the backstroke. Except for putts of two feet or less, I think this is an unnatural and hence a poor way to swing the club back because it produces a tendency to shove the club back rather than swing it. When you shove, you are apt to hood the blade and/or overinvolve the upper arms and shoulders in the stroke. In either case, you cannot develop the kind of repetitive action you need for correct speed and proper direction. With a pendulum-type stroke you can, and a pendulum-type stroke requires some *natural* raising of the club off the ground.

The amount the club raises depends on the length of the stroke, which in turn is dictated by the length of the putt. The longer the putt, of course, the higher the club will *naturally* raise off the ground.

With my descending putter head, however, the follow-through after impact is likely to be very short for putts under fifteen feet. Indeed, sometimes the blade will pretty much stop or even meet the ground after impact, and there is nothing wrong with it. On longer putts, the blade will raise up in the follow-through, naturally, without any special effort on your part.

THE TEMPO—ANYTHING BUT FAST

A pendulum stroke, by definition, is a rhythmic stroke. Its opposite is the so-called pop stroke, which features a very short backswing and a quick, sharp, jabbing impact, with a follow-through usually much longer, proportionally, than the backswing. The pop stroke doesn't make music, it makes a bang. The pendulum stroke might be likened, in musical terms, to a fox trot. The tempo is relaxed and slow. In fact, I don't think a putter can be swung too slowly, *especially going back, which is where the tempo for the entire stroke is determined.*

The best putters in the game, with very few exceptions, have had a very *deliberate* take-away. Jack Nicklaus is the prime example of this. Jack has said he stands over a putt as long as he does before stroking because he is waiting until he senses he is totally ready to move the club. I believe that this getting ready is tied up with his slow backstroke: he's waiting for the tension to drain from his arms and hands so he can take the club away smoothly and slowly. When you swing a putter back slowly, you have full control of the clubhead and that brings smoothness.

In a true pendulum stroke the putter essentially just drops *down on the ball*, like an acorn free-falling from an oak tree. It may appear there is no acceleration at impact, but only to those not accustomed to seeing a truly evenly paced putting stroke. The majority of golfers, it seems to me, make too short a backstroke—I believe because they feel this is the best way to keep the blade on line. Then, understandably, they think they must give the ball a little extra hit to get it to the hole.

The result is rarely smooth, and frequently the ball goes the wrong distance and well wide of the hole.

People tell me that better nerves are needed to putt my way than to pop putt. I think they are dead wrong. You need good (that is, calm) nerves to putt well any way you choose, but a short jab stroke can only get faster and jabbier the more the nerves get into the act. If you *expect* to take the clubhead back a comfortable distance, allowing your instincts to determine how far, then the chances are pretty good that you'll make a slower, rhythmic pass at the ball. If you tell yourself to make an artificially short backstroke, then it will more than likely be a fast one. As far as I'm concerned, in putting, speed of stroke definitely kills.

"TURNING ON"—THE IGNITION

Is there a specially effective way to start the putting stroke in the first place? This is a central problem in golf, be it for full shots or putting, because we must begin from a stationary situation—a still body and a still ball. The most common way to get moving, in putting as in full shotmaking, is the forward press—easing the hands slightly targetward just before beginning the stroke.

The forward press does help to promote a descending blow, but I'm basically against it for two reasons. First, it can and often does change the loft of the putter. Second, it can cause the blade to open or close before the club is drawn back. Thus, if you use the forward press, you should adjust your stance and line to accommodate these effects on your action.

Another ignition key, equally common as the forward

42

43

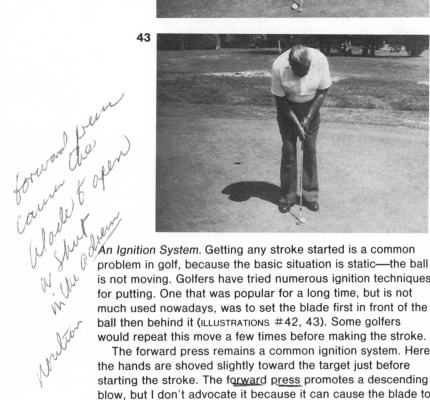

An Ignition System. Getting any stroke started is a common problem in golf, because the basic situation is static—the ball is not moving. Golfers have tried numerous ignition techniques for putting. One that was popular for a long time, but is not much used nowadays, was to set the blade first in front of the ball then behind it (ILLUSTRATIONS #42, 43). Some golfers would repeat this move a few times before making the stroke.

The forward press remains a common ignition system. Here the hands are shoved slightly toward the target just before starting the stroke. The forward press promotes a descending blow, but I don't advocate it because it can cause the blade to open or shut in the address position (ILLUSTRATIONS #44, 45).

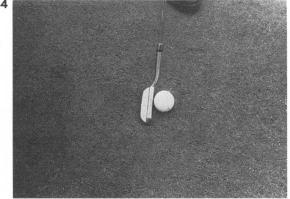

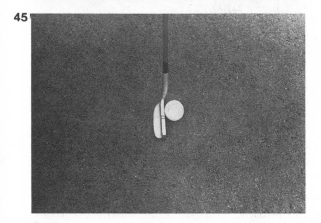

press, is the waggle. This can take different forms. Some golfers will set the blade in front of the ball, then behind it, repeating this maneuver a few times. Others will move the putter back and forth behind the ball the way a pool shooter does his cue before stroking. In either case, you would do well to begin the stroke very soon after the last waggle to get full value from it.

Personally, I'm not much for waggling. I think it can throw out the face alignment, and maybe the concentration. I recall Tommy Armour waggling as many as twenty times before hitting a putt, and the oddest thing was that he never looked at the ball while doing so. I think he did this so as to not be intimidated by the ball—not to become ball-fixated—but that's just a guess.

Anyway, I prefer getting into position after my rehearsal stroke, then letting it go. Too much waiting around over the ball can only breed tension—except, it seems, in a guy like Nicklaus. But then Nicklaus has always been something special in the game.

ONLY THE LINE CHANGES

The path of the putting stroke is a *constant*.

No matter if you have a side-hiller or a straight putt, you do not alter the stroke but aim the club accordingly. This is what is meant by the remark, "Every putt is a straight putt," which I endorse all the way. If you have a putt that you figure breaks three inches, you simply hit a straight putt to that point where you think it will begin to turn.

Of course, figuring where to aim is one of the great challenges in putting, which makes it worth a separate chapter.

PLAYING THE GRAIN

There is more to counteracting grain than getting a true reading of it.

For example, on putts over twenty-five feet the grain for the first ten feet or so is not going to affect the break of the ball because it will be moving with too much force. However, as the ball slows down the grain definitely will be a factor. So, on longer putts, in making your prestroke calculations, check mainly the grain within a few feet of the cup. On putts under twenty-five feet, and especially within ten or so feet of the cup, carefully consider the grain from beginning to end.

Here's another grain factor often overlooked by poor putters. While thicker-textured grasses such as Bermuda will have a lot of grain, you shouldn't allow as much break as you might think, because these greens are usually slower running and thus the ball must be hit harder to reach the cup, which reduces the effect of grain.

There is no foolproof, scientific way to determine how much to allow for the effects of grain in any given green. It is a matter of guesswork at first, which becomes educated guesswork as you gain more experience with grain on a particular course, or in a particular region. If there is any one factor you can count on, it is that the faster a ball rolls, the less effect the grain will have *on side–hill–breaking putts.* With this in mind my advice on unfamiliar greens is to allow for a minimum amount of break while hitting your putts firmer—to putt "through the grain," as the saying goes. Of course, on very quick-running greens you need to be careful in this regard but, then, grain is never as much of a factor on really slick surfaces.

READING THE SLOPE

To any calculation of the grain must be added the slope or contour of the ground itself. For example, if the slope is from right to left and the grain runs from left to right, your line of putt must be a balance between these two elements. Chances are, the putt will be pretty much straight if the slope is not severe and the grain is not especially heavy.

Unfortunately, reading the slopes of greens is a lot more difficult than reading grain. Contouring can be very subtle and almost indiscernible to the naked eye, particularly in old greens thirty to fifty years of age that have been subject to the shifting of earth.

Many golfers like to assess the break of a putt by looking at the line from both ends—from the ball to the hole, and from the hole back to the ball. Some will also look from side-on to the line. Maybe I'm old-fashioned, but I believe all those angles only confuse the issue and that you are better off going with what you see from directly behind your ball.

I do think, though, that it's a good idea to assess the overall slope of the entire green area from a distance, ideally as you first walk up and onto the putting surface. Use this information to confirm what you see when you get down to perceiving the details of the specific piece of ground you will be putting over.

THE TELL-TALE HOLE

Another way to find the direction of slope is to check the cup itself. If you know there is some roll in the region of the hole but are not sure of which way it goes, look into the hole and see how much earth there is between the top of the sunken cup and the very top of the hole. Assuming the hole has been cut properly, the side showing the most earth will be on the high side, and the slope will be away from it.

In the end, however, judging how much break to play is always something of a guessing game—a combination of picking the right line along which to aim the putt and hitting the ball to it at the correct speed.

THE SPEED FACTOR

A straight-in downhill or uphill putt takes no fancy consideration. You simply stroke the ball softer or harder, and hopefully on line. For uphill putts that break right or left, you generally should not allow as much borrow as on downhill-breaking putts, because you will be hitting the ball more firmly. Conversely, on downhill breakers you borrow more, because you are going to hit the ball more softly. This is what is meant by "speed putting," a phrase heard so much on golf telecasts.

On level putts with some break in one direction or another, when you're not sure how much to borrow, do as I suggested in the same situation with grain: hit the ball firmly and more directly at the hole—"putt through the break," or, to use another term meaning the same thing, "take the break out of the putt."

How do you determine the speed of greens? Except for the factor of the grain being with or against you, there is very little science involved. Judging speed is almost entirely a question of feel—feel you get through your feet (just walking on a green will tell you something of how fast it is running), by watching the putts of your playing partners, and by your own experience. If, as you always should, you use the practice putting green before a round, and it's in the same condition as the course greens, that's a big help. Otherwise, all you can really do is hope for the best on the first green of the round, then pick up a sense of speed from that.

You must also keep in mind that, when you begin a round early in the morning, the greens will be slower than an hour or so later, because of dew. This is true even if the greens have been swept, because of the remaining dampness. If the greens are of Bermuda grass, the grass on a hot day will be growing pretty quickly, so thay may be slow from dew early in the morning, faster from say the sixth through the fourteenth holes, then a little slower from there on in.

Remember, too, that wind always dries out greens, making them faster running.

PICK YOUR SPOT

On breaking putts, which I am inclined to think are in the majority, you first have to read grain and slope and judge the speed of the green. Finally, you have to decide where the ball will begin to curve toward the hole. In this regard, way too may golfers have only a vague notion of the point where the break will begin. Mostly, they are too "hole conscious"—like aiming a torpedo at a ship without figuring in its movement through the water.

What you should do is find some sort of mark on the green along the line of the putt as you have perceived it. Aim your putter at that spot, then concentrate your attention on it as you set up to and stroke the ball. This short target may be a slight discoloration in the grass, or an old pitch mark—anything that gives you a definite

Pick a Spot. Spot putting is very important to success on breaking putts. In effect, you play a straight putt by starting the ball directly at your selected spot. In this illustration of a left-to-right breaking putt, my spot is a small white mark on the green about halfway to the hole. Since it is an irregularity in the surface, the putt is played just inside it. I prefer a spot closer to the ball—around twelve to eighteen inches—but, if none is available, you go with what you can find.

aiming point. Whatever it may be, that spot becomes your real target. This is called "spot putting," and I am strongly in favor of it.

Some spot putters prefer to pick a point about half way down the length of the putt. I prefer picking a mark only twelve to eighteen inches in front of my ball if there is one, and, if not, as close as possible beyond that distance. This way I can bring the target very close to me, which makes it easier both to see and to hit, and also less intimidating. Once you're over the ball, visualize the entire line of the putt from the hole back to the ball, pick a close-up spot on that line, then go for it.

Finally, one small reservation about spot putting. Except on unusually sharp breakers, I don't think it's a good system for putts under about twelve feet or so. From this distance the target should be some part of the hole itself—the center, or the right edge, or the left edge. This is especially true on slow greens, where you need to stroke the ball very firmly.

CHAPTER 4

READING THE GREENS

READING THE GRAIN

The people who argue that putting and golf are two different games will also say, after that argument goes stale, that all greens should be perfectly flat. Ben Hogan was a proponent of this, and on the only golf course he ever built he put down eighteen pancakes. Of course, Hogan came to hate putting when he got that bad case of the yips.

Perfectly flat greens supposedly diminish the importance of putting, or at least the difficulty. However, even over a dead-flat surface you're going to have to hit the putt straight at the cup, and also at the right speed. Neither is automatic.

Then there's the factor that, even if all greens were built absolutely flat, people still wouldn't putt that way. The grain of the grass affects the direction a putted ball takes, and, except in very rare instances, all golf greens have *some* grain. Grain is formed by the direction in which the grass is growing—which way the blade tips point. If the tips lay to the right or left of the line of putt, the ball will roll toward them and you must allow for this. When the tips run in the direction of the putt, the ball will roll more swiftly than if they were facing the ball; in the latter case obviously you must hit it harder to overcome the resistance.

One way of finding the grain is to look at the grass from behind your ball. If it has a shiny look, you are going with the grain; if the grass has a dull appearance, you are putting into the grain. Unfortunately, if the sun isn't shining, or the grain is across the line of the putt, this method isn't going to be much help. Thus a backup way to read grain is to look for nearby lakes, ponds, or streams, because grass generally grows toward a main source of water. Also, grass usually grows *away from* the slope of a mountain, and *toward* the setting sun. Keep your eyes peeled for such factors as you walk onto greens.

CHAPTER 5

PICKING A PUTTER

KEEP IT SIMPLE

The huge variety of putters on the market, now and in the past, is testimony to the unique quality of the putting game. Individuality gets its fullest expression through putters of all shapes and sizes—some looking to me like certain household appliances or exotic plumbers' tools. All I can say about this is that the best golfers, and especially the great putters, have almost always used putters of a simple, straightforward design, be they mallet-headed or blades.

There is no doubt that the appearance of a putter is very important to the player's performance with it, and this is probably the most persuasive factor in the choice of a "wand," even more than balance or feel. Actually, the same thing pertains to picking a driver, a wedge, or a set of irons, and this is understandable because golfers have a very intimate relationship with their clubs.

I know everyone sees things a little differently, but it seems to me that the cleaner the lines of a putter, the less complicated its look and the more comfortable it appears, the less distracting it will be to the player. To each his own, but my advice in choosing a putter is to keep it simple in overall design.

As for specific construction features, the only thing I suggest is a putter with a little offset: that is, the blade located a little behind the shaft—to the golfer's right of it—or what used to be called a "gooseneck." I think the offset makes it easier to line up putts, because it automatically sets the hands a little ahead of the putter blade.

. . . AND HEAVY

I am more categorical when it comes to what I regard as the really important elements in putters, those being weight, grip, and lie. Of course, my recommendations here relate directly to my own method of putting, but that's exactly as it should be.

First of all, I believe it is imperative that a putter be fairly heavy—of an overall weight around seventeen or eighteen ounces, but with the head weight more pronounced. This is because you can get a lot more feel with weight at the end of a stick than when the weight is equally distributed from top to bottom. I am asking you to develop a rhythmic, pendulum-type stroke, with the clubhead more or less dropping down on the ball, and this is most easily achieved with a heavy-headed putter.

With a light putter you have to cultivate more of a *hitting* stroke, which leaves most golfers open to misdirecting the club. With a light putter it is also harder to obtain a consistent feel, especially on those days when your nerves are not as calm as they might be or your hands just don't have that nice thin feeling. Then you have to take a firmer hold on the club, which further reduces your feel. With a heavy-headed putter, you can use that weight instead of the hands to stroke the ball. Another advantage of the heavier putter is that it makes you less susceptible to a short, quick stroke, which leads to the yips.

GRIP THIN, LIE LOW

Again, for maximum feel, the putter grip should be thin *no matter the size of an individual's hands.* Of course, there is no specific degree of thinness for all golfers, and hand size does have some say in this. On the whole, however, you do not want a fat grip, because a thin one *always* produces more head feel—try it and see. As for grip material, leather is always good, but the choice is a matter of personal preference.

As I noted, I want my hands to be low at address, with the club extended from my body at around a forty-five-degree angle. In golf terminology, this calls for a putter with a "flat" lie. Isao Aoki is the most obvious example of what I mean by being flat at address, and he also happens to be one of the best putters in the game. The exact degree of flatness obviously varies from person to person depending on height and build, and you'll probably need to experiment to find a putter that suits you perfectly (or bend one to the desired lie). The most important thing is that you don't get into a situation where you must adjust your stance to a particular putter. Make the putter fit you.

There is a lot of comment about the way Aoki's putter

blade sticks up in the air at the toe, but, as far as I'm concerned, so what! Aoki is simply taking that part of the putter he never uses out of play by hitting the ball with the strongest part of the club, where the shaft and head join. This is the same as hitting the ball on or toward the heel with other types of putters. Aoki might have gotten a putter with a rocker sole that would have allowed the head to sit on the ground the way putters usually do, but he didn't and, to my mind, there's no reason why he should have.

By the way, you can find the sweet spot by a simple test. Hold the grip with your fingertips at the very top, letting the club dangle easily. With the index finger of your other hand make a short, sharp poke at a point near the center of the blade. If the head goes backward from this poke squarely, without the toe or heel flaring inward or outward, you've found the sweet spot. You may have to make a few pokes before finding the spot, and you'll often find it's not where the manufacturer has put a line or mark.

THE LOFT STORY

Prior to the 1960s, before the tremendous improvements in the surfaces of greens, most putters had as much as eight degrees of loft. Greens were not nearly as uniformly smooth as now, and you needed loft to get the ball "on top of the grass" right away for a fair roll.

Modern-day putters are made with about three degrees of loft, and I know of some with none at all. Loft, therefore, is a consideration in choosing a putter, and not the least in that it gives the blade a certain look. If you don't like the look, but go for the club for other reasons, you can always play the ball a little more forward—toward your left foot—and you won't see the loft. However, as you should know by now, I would not recommend that.

To my way of thinking, the loft on a putter doesn't mean a whole lot, simply because only a pinpoint amount of the clubface is actually contacting the ball (the time the ball and clubface spend together is a matter of milliseconds). Therefore, I can't see how loft can have much effect on a putt, particularly if you putt with a descending blow, and thus catch the ball near the top of the blade.

MATERIAL MATTERS

I don't go along with the idea that hickory shafts give more of a feel, or a better feel, for putting than steel. On the other hand, I don't think hickory gives any worse or lesser feel. However, if *you* think hickory, or graphite, or anything else, is better, then go ahead and use it. In the psychology of putting the golfer's mental attitude is definitely affected by things that may have no physical effect on his performance, such as shaft material or the sound of the club when it hits the ball. I personally like to use a putter head of soft steel because it feels and sounds better—softer—to me, especially with a balata-cover ball. (To me, surlyn gives off an uncomfortably hard, rocky sound.)

KEEP YOUR GLOVE ON

Many golfers who wear a golf glove remove it for putting. It seems to me that by doing so they are breaking up the continuity of feel for the club, even though they are going from hard-hit full shots to the much softer stroke of putting. I don't wear a golf glove, and I wouldn't dream of using one to putt, but I think it should work the other way around, too.

STICK TO YOUR GUN

It is a lot easier to change putters than a set of woods or irons, if only because buying one club is not as big a strain on the wallet. Thus golfers are prone to spend money on new putters, hoping they will improve the situation. It often happens, too, that when a golfer gets on a hot run, be he a touring pro or a player at your club, people get very interested in using the kind of equipment he is using. You see that a lot among the tour pros, particularly. I remember once when Jug McSpaden came out with a twenty-four-ounce putter with a big gooseneck and a hickory shaft. It was an ugly looking, ungainly thing, but he started holing everything, and in no time at all everyone was looking for the same sort of club.

Certainly there are always enough different kinds of putters to choose from, but in my experience all the great putters in the game have tended to stick with the same putter throughout their career. Among them I think of Bobby Jones and his Calamity Jane, a thin-bladed putter; Bobby Locke, who used a putter very much like Jones's; Walter Hagen and his very heavy blade; and Lloyd Mangrum and Billy Casper with their very similar mallet-head putters. I believe they stuck with the same putter because they were not looking for an easy out when their putting did occasionally go sour. They understood that it isn't the putter but the fellow holding it that makes the difference. So get a putter that feels and looks good, and stick with it through thick and thin.

When your putting goes bad, more often than not it is your tempo that has changed, and another putter is not going to solve that problem. This is why I also don't go along with the idea of changing putters for different types of greens—a heavy one for slow greens, a light one for fast greens, and so on. When you change putters this way you must also change your tempo to allow for a different weight and feel. It is a lot easier to adjust to greens with your familiar putter than to adjust to *both* a new putter *and* new greens. If the greens are slower than customary, simply swing the putter a little bit harder. Above all, use the same putter on every type of surface—and make sure it's *heavy.*

CHAPTER 6

PRACTICE

. . . *UNTIL IT HURTS*

I have made a very strong statement already about the
need to practice putting, and to practice it a lot. I am no
different in this respect from any other golf professional.
It takes no special genius to know that practice is the
only way anybody finally gets better at anything. At the
same time, though, I will admit that practicing putting
is not easy on your body. In fact, mainly because of the
static bending-over position required, putting practice
can on the whole be even more strenuous than hitting
irons and woods.

Henry Cotton will tell you that. As a young man the
great British champion-to-be would practice putting for
hours at a time, and as a result eventually suffered a severe back ailment. Raymond Floyd, the outstanding
American touring pro, uses an extra long putter precisely to avoid what happened to Cotton. He says he can
practice putting a lot longer because he doesn't have to
bend so much—and Floyd does practice a lot.

Okay, you should not practice for so long at a time
that you hurt yourself physically. Nor should you prac-

tice past the point where your concentration is lost and you find yourself hitting a lot of putts with no purpose or thought behind them. Practice for as long as you comfortably can at every session, but have a lot of sessions. If you have a golf club with a putting clock convenient to you, it's a lot less trouble to go out in the late afternoon and hit putts for a while than to whack out a couple of buckets of full shots.

Indeed, you can practice putting without a golf course or a putting clock. There is nothing at all wrong with hitting putts on a carpet at home, so long as it is fairly close in smoothness to a grass green.

Wherever you practice, at every session work on something specific—grip, alignment, posture, stroke path, tempo, right-to-left and left-to-right putts, or whatever. This, of course, is how you maintain concentration and make every practice session count.

LET THE MIRROR DO THE TALKING

All the above is elementary advice about putting practice. There are also some specific ideas I recommend that may or may not be unique but which I have found valuable over the years. One is to use a full-length mirror placed wherever in your home you can hit putts. Putt facing the mirror directly, and also putt standing sideways to it. Put a ball down, set the putter behind it, set up the way you do normally, then look in the mirror as you make your stroke.

You don't have to watch the ball to hit it—you can see its reflection in the mirror. The advantage of this

Mirror, Mirror . . . The one practice I recommend that is unique is the one where you use a mirror to check your body and blade alignment and your stroke. The advantage is you don't have to rely on the perspective or language of someone else to judge or assess what you are doing.

practice method is that you don't need anyone to tell you what you are or are not doing with your putting. You are not subject to another person's perspective or language, which can be easily misinterpreted or simply not well understood. With the mirror you can develop your technique, and then continually check yourself out, entirely in your own language, so to speak.

TEES AND STRIPES, AND LEFT HAND ONLY

Another way to sharpen your putting, and make a practice session fun, is to put a tee in the green and use it as the target, trying to hit it. This is a good exercise just before playing a round, because when you get on the golf course the holes are going to look nice and big to you.

In order to check if you are getting true end-over-end roll on your putts, use a ball with a painted stripe on it, or set an unstriped ball with its name facing upward. You will know right away if you are cutting or hooking your putts. When the ball is properly stroked, the stripe won't waver, while the ball name will appear like a roller on a slot machine.

In order to strengthen the concept of the left hand being the rudder in the putting stroke, hit a lot of practice putts holding the putter only with the left hand. The grip should be weak, as it is when both hands are on the club. The idea here, of course, is to reaffirm the idea that the left hand must not break down, or cock targetward, in the forward stroke. Chances are that if you do this exercise enough, you will actually strengthen that left hand and make it even less susceptible to breaking down.

PUTT FOR DOUGH

In view of my reputation as a man who likes to putt for a few bucks, I should tell you that putting on the practice green with someone for money is a good way to sharpen up. And that is exactly what I will tell you, and mean it. There is nothing wrong with a little gambling on your ability. It doesn't have to be for very much money—just a little something to "make it interesting," as the old saying goes.

VARIETY IS THE SPICE OF PUTTING

It has been suggested that a good way to perfect your putting stroke is to find a putt you know well on the practice green and play it over and over again. The idea is that, since you know the roll and have a sense of the distance, you can forget these factors and concentrate only on the stroke itself.

I don't believe there is much merit to this idea. You may start making a lot of that one putt, but you will be developing a false sense of confidence. No two putts are ever quite alike, each needs a reading and its own alignment, and this variety should be simulated in your practice putting sessions.

I have only one qualifier on this matter. I think most of your practice putts should be in the four- and five-foot range. From these distances you best develop the pendulum-type stroke wherein you simply let the clubhead do the work, which is the ideal kind of stroke to have. At four or five feet there is not much hitting involved. Of course, you should practice medium- and long-range putts, too, but the concentration should be on the shorter ones.

PUT THE FEEL BACK

If you hit fifty or maybe one hundred balls on the practice range before playing a round, it is very important that you hit some practice putts before teeing off. When you hit a lot of full shots in quick succession, your hands will swell up to a certain extent from the accumulated work load you have placed on them. You must give them time to get back to normal, and you can accomplish that, while also putting some sensitivity back in your hands, by hitting practice putts for ten or so minutes before you tee off.

YIPS AWAY

Everyone has had or will someday have the yips, which is a nervous twitch that was supposed to be a putting stroke. I have had them, but I developed a way to get rid of them. In the address position I tighten my forearms as I would if I were showing off my muscles, and also crouch down a little more. With these changes, all I can do is shove the ball: hand action is practically eliminated.

That is not the way I expect to putt normally, but it is better than the short, quick jab that is the yip stroke. Of course, when I sense the yips have gone for a while, I go back to my regular putting style.

In the end, though, because the yips come from a fear of missing putts, usually the short ones, the best way to overcome them is to *make* a lot of those putts. The best place to start making them is on the practice putting green. It is here where you find and perfect your most effective putting stroke, as well as a putting procedure and a genuine feel for this important part of the game. From this comes the confidence that you know what you are doing, and it's just such confidence that will keep away the dreaded yips.

No fear, no yips.

CHAPTER 7

THE STYLES OF THE BEST

A look at the styles of the game's best putters quickly reveals that no two do it quite the same way. The same thing holds for full golf swings, of course, despite the greater degree of standardization that has come to this part of the game.

Still, it is worth considering the various ways fine golfers have devised to putt the ball into the hole. Since there is such a variety of styles, it stands to reason that any golfer can borrow a little something from a variety of other players and be better off for it.

I may not agree with some of the methods I will describe, but that doesn't mean they are wrong . . . or that I am.

BOBBY JONES

Jones had a rhythmic stroke that matched his full–shotmaking style. He had a fairly long putting stroke that definitely moved to the inside on the way back, and I recall he gave the club a touch of a roll with the right hand at impact.

Jones set his feet quite close together, with the left foot open a hair, and his weight very definitely on his left side. He took the club back with his left hand, hit the ball with his right hand, and did not think the follow-through was very important. That's because he hit the ball with a descending blow.

It should be obvious that Jones was my kind of putter.

WALTER HAGEN

There were times when Hagen took a wide stance, other times when it was very narrow. I think he favored the narrow stance most of the time, but, anyway, his varying the width is the mark of a man who goes with what feels good at the moment, rather than locking himself into one system. I think that was one of the problems with Ben Hogan when he got into the yips. He wouldn't try anything different, just kept fighting the nerves with the same medicine.

Hagen always kept his weight on the left side, though, and had a very slow stroke tempo. That was the key to his success on the greens: a long, slow backstroke to the inside of his target line, then a firm but measured forward stroke that brought the clubface back to square at impact.

BOBBY LOCKE

Most everyone who remembers Locke, a truly fabulous putter, talks of how he hooked every putt, with the blade actually closing at impact, giving the ball right-to-left sidespin. That wasn't the way I saw it. Locke did have a very closed stance, his body aimed well to the right of his line of putt, and he brought the club back on the same line as his body, so it, too, was well inside the line of putt on the backswing. From there, however, instead of the blade shutting as it swung back in order to send the ball on the desired line, Locke's right shoulder would move outward, or forward, or "over the top," just before he started his downstroke. It was this move that got the blade back to square at impact, *not* a turning over of his right hand.

Locke also had a very definite pause at the end of his backstroke, and it was this that allowed him to work his right shoulder as I've described and still keep control of the club.

LLOYD MANGRUM

The outstanding feature of Mangrum's putting action was his tempo. Mangrum was known for his slow backswing when hitting full shots, and it carried over to his putting, which, in fact, was his strongest suit. Mangrum also used a very long putter—around forty inches, almost the length of a driver—and I believe this was a factor in his tempo. If you've ever tried putting with a driver you'll know that the stroke has to be deliberate in pace, and usually pretty accurate. That's what Lloyd was after, and what he got.

Mangrum also kept his feet very close together and concentrated his weight on his left side, but, in a departure from what I like to see, he played the ball a little forward of his left heel.

ARNOLD PALMER

It may seem strange to list Arnold Palmer among the
best putters in the game, in view of the fact that he
eventually lost his touch on the greens. But he was very
good when he had it and is thus worth some analysis,
especially since he came to me for help fairly early in
his professional career.

A good bit of Arnie's technique when in his prime did
reflect my notion on the business of putting. He
crouched fairly low over the ball, kept his hands in close
to his body, and, with a distinctly wristy stroking action,
hit the ball on the downbeat. On the other hand, Palmer
never looked very comfortable over the ball. He was too
crunched up, too crowded. A lot of this came from the
knock-kneed stance he adopted to keep his body quiet
during the stroke. That was particularly important to

Arnie, because he was such an aggressive putter and needed to stand very still to get the solid hit and accuracy necessary to rush the hole as hard as he did.

This gets to the main difference between what I talk about and Palmer's prime-time putting method. Arnie's tempo was almost as fast as the swing he used for full shots. Efficiency over the long haul with that kind of upbeat putting stroke pace is difficult to maintain.

JACK NICKLAUS

Here again is a perfect example of what good tempo—that is, *slow* tempo—can mean to putting. Nicklaus has a very deliberate backstroke, even for the longest of putts, when, because of the extra force needed, the tendency is to go at the ball a little quicker. It may have been in his nature to be so deliberate, but it no doubt helped to have grown up on the smooth and fast greens of Scioto Country Club.

Jack also uses an open stance, and this makes it easier for him to get his right shoulder low behind the ball and his head in a position where he can look directly down the line of his putt. No peeking around the corner for Nicklaus. On the stroke itself, Jack uses his shoulders more than I think is good, but he manages to handle this because of his great tempo. He cocks his wrists some on the backstroke, but not on the downstroke, which he himself has described as a kind of shove at the ball.

BILLY CASPER

In certain important respects Casper putted the way I think is best. The movement was almost entirely from the elbows down (except on putts over twenty feet), and he struck the ball with a descending blow, in good part because he played it well inside his left heel.

Otherwise, I have never much liked the way Casper hoods the clubface swinging back, which calls for opening it through impact—a risky business unless you prac-

tice an awful lot. (Billy denies he hoods the club, and if in his mind he doesn't, fine, but he was always one of the most diligent practicers of putting.) Casper has more of a pop or tap stroke than most, which means an abrupt sort of punch at the ball. I'm not especially fond of that, but in this case it comes from an idiosyncrasy of his, namely, keeping the hands so close to the body that on the forward stroke the left hand's forward motion is stopped by the inside of his left leg. That leg serves as a guard, a barrier against the left hand breaking down.

One thing I have always liked about Casper's style is his lack of hesitation. He makes up his mind about what he wants to do with each putt, then goes after it without delay. That's the best way I know to beat the yips—or better still, never get them.

TOM WATSON

It could be that Tom Watson will be the "greatest putter in the game" only so long as he is on his hot run of victories, whereas a Bobby Locke or Billy Casper retains that reputation well after his prime competitive years. I say this only because Watson's overall putting tempo tends to be rather quick, which in my mind is not as sustaining as the slow tempo.

Then again, Tom is very conscious of sometimes being too fast a swinger of the club, and it is interesting that when he won his first U.S. Open (in 1982), which was a very important personal achievement, those who study such things recognized that Watson's swing tempo was just a tad slower. Which is to say, he is capable of revving down.

I speak of his swing tempo with drivers and irons, but it goes for his putting as well, for Watson's game is all of a piece.

He has become capable of slowing down at least his putting tempo, by developing a less wristy style than he once had. There is some cock in his wrists, but the basic action is arms and shoulders. Tom also stands fairly erect at the ball, which brings him up close to it and promotes a stroke that is more straight-back, straight-through than inside-to-square. Here again this is not what I profess as best, but, just as a descending blow saves Casper's hooded blade, Watson's slower tempo, when he has it, keeps him in line and to the cup.

GEORGE ARCHER

It is valuable to include George Archer in a roundup analysis of best putters, because we are seeing an increase in the overall size of young golfers, and so far George has been the best putter ever for a man of his great height (6' 6").

The main problem for tall golfers—as shotmakers as well as putters—is to stand steady. George solves this by accentuating the flex of his knees and the bend at his waist, which is also why he does not use an extra-long putter. He has described his position as "sitting in a chair," or being in the position just before actually taking the seat. He's right. We are usually very steady in that position, although we may not notice it because it passes so quickly as we go to sit down.

George places a big premium on no body movement, for good reason, and this more or less dictates the rest of his putting style. His is basically a stiff-wristed stroke, with a heavy dominance of the left hand. There's no wrist cock at all, the club being swung back and through pretty much square all the way by a movement of the upper arms and shoulders. It's not my cup of tea, as you know by now, but I can't knock it because it works well for George.

BEN CRENSHAW

I must admit that Ben Crenshaw is in many ways the antithesis of what I advocate for putting. He stands tall at the ball, is all arms and shoulders (although there is a slight wrist cock on his backstroke), and the ball is set pretty much toward his left toe so he hits it very close to on the upbeat. And yet, Crenshaw has the same sort of touch stroke, overall, that I like. I think this is because he has a pair of "soft" hands on the handle, plus a smooth, rhythmic stroke.

Ben is a great putter of his time, like Nicklaus, having grown up on smooth, fast greens.